SING A SONG OF CHRISTMAS

A CANTATA

BY MICHAEL BARRETT & JOSEPH M. MARTIN

ORCHESTRATION BY STAN PETHEL

CONTENTS

Performance Time: Approximately 25-30 min.

① This symbol indicates a track number on the StudioTrax CD or SplitTrax CD.

GlorySound

Visit Shawnee Press Online at
www.shawneepress.com

FOREWORD

The music of Christmas is a miracle of melody and message. On the wings of song, the good news of Christ's birth animates our dreams and sets our spirit's soaring. When we gather as community to contemplate grace and celebrate life, there is always music.

Sometimes the sounds are sweet and soft as a mother's lullaby. Then, without warning, angel choirs surprise and delight us, suddenly bursting forth with jubilant shouts and clarion acclamations. Listening and learning we find comfort and inspiration in these sacred canticles.

Our beloved carols connect us with the foundations of our faith even as our new songs of the season reach out to encourage those who will follow. In each note rests the assurance of hope, and in each phrase breathes the spirit of promise. When truth and tune are bonded together, each anthem can bring us closer to the peace, love and joy at the very heart of our spiritual quest.

When adoration moves us towards authentic worship and we think upon all of the wonders this season brings… how can we keep from singing?

JOSEPH M. MARTIN

PRELUDE OF JOY

Tune: **ANTIOCH**
by GEORGE FREDERICK HANDEL (1685-1759)
Arranged by
JOSEPH M. MARTIN (BMI)

A SONG OF CHRISTMAS

Words by
J. PAUL WILLIAMS (ASCAP)

Music by
JOSEPH M. MARTIN (BMI)

Come and sing a song of Christ-mas. Sing a song of Je-sus' birth.

Come and sing a song of Christ-mas. Come and praise Him, all the earth.

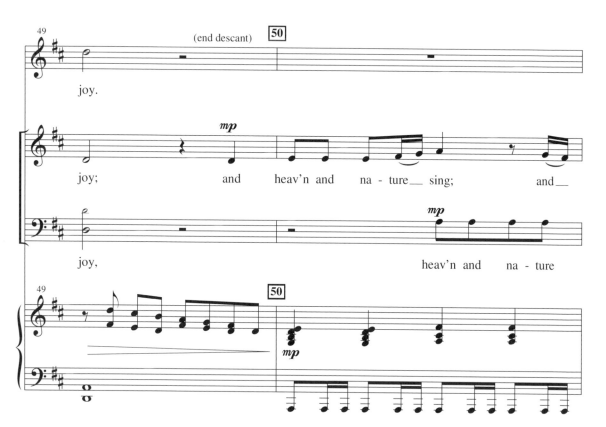

14

NARRATION:

The time for singing has come! Today on the wings of song we declare the wondrous season of joy, peace and light. With overflowing hearts we sing to share the timeless story of God's love and unfailing grace. From ancient times, the music of faith has carried this hopeful message from generation to generation. The prophets of old looked into the Scriptures searching for words of promise and encouragement. They cried out to God with deep longing for a Savior. The music of their impassioned prayers echoes still today in every seeker's heart.

COME, EMMANUEL

Words:
Latin Hymn

Tunes:
COVENTRY CAROL
GREENSLEEVES
Arranged by
MICHAEL BARRETT (BMI)

come, O come,____ Em - man - u - el,____ and ran - som cap - tive

* Tune: COVENTRY CAROL, Traditional English Melody
** Tune: GREENSLEEVES, Traditional English Melody
Words: Latin Hymn, tr. John Mason Neale, 1818-1866

18

joice, re - joice!___ Em - man - u - el,___ the prom - ised Son___ of

Da - vid.

* O come, Thou Wis - dom

from on high,___ and or - der all___ things far and nigh.

To

* Words: Latin Hymn, tr. Henry Sloane Coffin, 1877-1954

SING A SONG OF CHRISTMAS - SA(T)B

us the path___ of knowl - edge show,___ and cause___ us in___ Thy

ways___ to go. Re - joice, re - joice!___ Em - man - u - el___ shall

come to thee,___ O Is - ra - el! Re - joice, re - joice!___ Em -

man - u - el,___ the prom - ised Son___ of Da - vid.

cresc. poco a poco

O

come, De - sire___ of na - tions, bind___ all peo - ple in___ one

heart and mind. Bid en - vy, strife___ and quar - rels cease.___ Fill

all of the world___ with heav - en's peace. Re - joice, re - joice!___ Em -

man - u - el___ shall come to thee,___ O Is - ra - el! Re -

joice, re-joice! Em-man-u-el, the prom-ised Son of Da-vid. O come, Em-man-u-el.

NARRATION:

"Prepare the way of the Lord. Make straight in the desert a highway for our God." The prophet Isaiah called the people of the covenant to remember God's promise and to repent. Like a song in the night, His words brought both challenge and encouragement to the nation. We too must prepare our hearts to receive the blessings of God's grace. Let us empty our hearts of the noisy clamor of the world and listen for the sounds of Christ's coming. Let us all make straight the path and prepare the way with praise.

PREPARE THE WAY

Words and music by
MICHAEL BARRETT (BMI)
Incorporating tune:
NÖEL NOUVELET
Traditional French Melody

Sing we now the prom - ise! Christ is__ com - ing soon!

Sing we out in glad - ness! Christ is__ com - ing soon!

* Tune: NÖEL NOUVELET, Traditional French Melody

Make a joy-ful noise. Lift high your heart and voice. Sing we now Ho-san-na! Christ is___ com-ing soon!

19 **With a light jazz feel (♩ = ca. 126)**

des - ert___ a high - way for___ our God. Pre -

des - ert___ a high - way for___ our God.

pare the way___ of the Lord. Pre - pare the way___ of the

Pre - pare the way___ of the Lord. Pre -

Lord. Make straight in___ the des - ert___ a

pare___ the___ way. Make straight in___ the des - ert___ a

CALL THE BABY JESUS

Words and music by
MICHAEL BARRETT (BMI)
and JOSEPH M. MARTIN (BMI)

* Any voice.

NARRATION:

When it was near time for Mary to deliver her Child, she and Joseph traveled to Bethlehem to register for the census. The town was crowded and the couple could not find a place for the night. At last they found shelter in a rustic stable, and it was in this humble setting the "Light of the World" was born. There in that simple, hay-filled manger, Mary placed her Baby, this perfect Lamb sent from the very heart of God.

to the members of the Bee Cave Sanctuary Choir,
Bee Cave Baptist Church, Bee Cave, Texas

SLEEP, LITTLE LAMB

Words and music by
JOSEPH M. MARTIN (BMI)

In the cold of win-ter, on a cloud-less

44

SING A SONG OF CHRISTMAS - SA(T)B

cresc.

Ten-der-ly we lift our songs to the new-born

King. One day loud ho - san - nas

will praise the great I Am;_____ but to-night, hearts

Ten-der-ly we lift our songs to the new-born King. One day loud ho-san - nas will praise the great I Am;＿＿＿＿＿ but to-night, hearts

50

whis - per, "Sleep, lit - tle__ Lamb;"

but to-night hearts whis - per, "Sleep, lit - tle__

Lamb."

morendo

NARRATION:

Later that same evening, in the Judean hill country, a group of shepherds kept watch over their flocks. Dozing in the coolness of the evening, they were suddenly awakened by a loud shout from the skies. A legion of angels had gathered to announce the birth of the Savior, calling into the night, "Glory to God in the highest and peace to all of goodwill." The shepherds went rejoicing to find the newborn King as the hillsides rang with the music of praise.

COME, HEAR THE MUSIC

Words by
J. PAUL WILLIAMS (ASCAP)

Music by
JOSEPH M. MARTIN (BMI)

54

NARRATION:

During this miraculous time God placed a beautiful star in the heavens as a sacred sign. Bethlehem was bathed in heaven's glory, and many saw this dazzling light and wondered. In the east, stargazers were amazed at the sight. These Magi were drawn to follow this celestial sign in search of divine truth. For many months they travelled until they found Jesus, the Bright and Morning Star. As a sign of devotion and praise, they gave Him precious gifts and then worshiped Him. From Bethlehem to the far corners of the earth, God's light was beginning to shine with hope and grace.

IN BETHLEHEM

Words by
BILLY D. MARTIN

Music by
JOSEPH M. MARTIN (BMI)

dark-ness sur-ren - dered to glo-ri-ous light.___

E - ven the shad-ows looked to the skies___ and took flight.___

The Morn-ing Star___ had come,___

God's on - ly Son___ in Beth - le - hem.

62

shout - ed the news___ all a - round.___ The Liv - ing

Word___ had come,___ God's on - ly Son,___ in Beth - le -

hem. In Beth - le - hem,___ a star was

shin - ing a - bove.

In Beth - le - hem,___ a song was born.

In Beth - le - hem,___ God gave His prom - ise of love,___

unis.

a love that lasts for - ev - er -

In Beth - le - hem,__ a Sav - ior was born.__

Sor - row sur - ren - dered to peace ev - er - more,__

NARRATION:

The light that shone on Bethlehem so many years ago is still shining for us today. Seekers still follow its flame and discover new life. The faithful still gather by candlelight to remember and declare their worship and devotion.

And so now, with hearts rejoicing, we lift our carols of praise.

With spirits united, we proclaim our thanksgiving and commitment to Christ.

With voices raised in song, we share what we believe.

Christ the Promise was born.

Christ the Teacher lived.

Christ the Savior died.

Christ the Lord rose again.

Christ the King will come again in glory.

Rejoice!
Glory to God in the Highest!

Alleluia!
Let the song of Christmas resound!

CHRISTMAS SONGS OF JOY

Additional words by
MICHAEL BARRETT (BMI)

Tunes:
ADESTE FIDELES
McCRAY
HYFRYDOL
Arranged by
MICHAEL BARRETT (BMI)

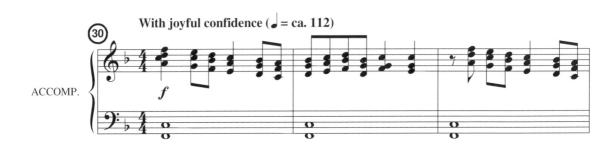

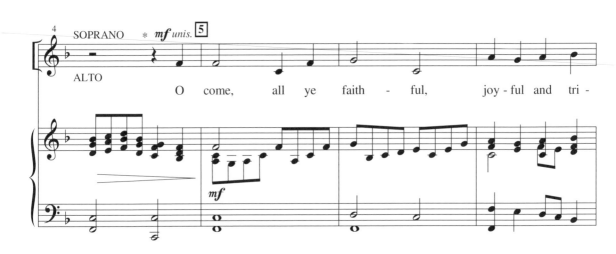

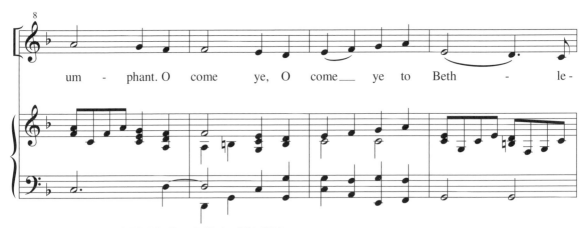

* Tune: ADESTE FIDELES, John Francis Wade, 1711-1786
  Words: Latin Hymn, ascribed to John Francis Wade, 1711-1786; tr. Frederick Oakley, 1802-1880

70

glo - ry, al - le - lu - ia, glo - ry, al - le - lu - ia. Je - sus Christ is

born___ to - day.

Come, all peo - ple,

* Tune: HYFRYDOL, Rowland H. Prichard, 1811-1887
Words: Michael Barrett (BMI)

SING A SONG OF CHRISTMAS - SA(T)B

MORE RESOURCES FOR THE DEVELOPING CHOIR

IN CHRIST ALONE

ACOUSTIC PRAISE FOR THE GROWING CHOIR

Keith Getty/Kristyn Getty/ Stuart Townend

The increasing treasury of modern hymns and sacred songs by Keith and Kristyn Getty and collaborator Stuart Townend are explored in this new resource designed for choirs of any level. Many of this writing team's biggest successes are included – all lovingly adapted by some of our most gifted arrangers. There is music for the entire church year contained in this collection. Transcending stylistic boundaries, the music and message are home in both contemporary-styled worship venues and traditional programs. Creative instrumental adornments offer additional options for performance while sensitive arranging make this compilation accessible to choirs of any size.

35028876	SAB	$9.95
35028877	Listening CD	$15.99
35028878	Preview Pack (Book/Listening CD)	$14.99
35028879	10-Pack Listening CDs	$59.99
35028880	Instrumental CD-ROM	$59.95
35028881	StudioTrax CD	$49.99
35028882	SplitTrax CD	$49.99

SING A SONG OF CHRISTMAS

Michael Barrett/Joseph M. Martin

Written especially for developing choirs, this festive SA(T)B cantata is overflowing with joyful seasonal songs ideal for smaller ensembles. Original material mingles with traditional carols in a jubilant mix, crafted to create large musical impact with minimal numbers and rehearsal time. The musical variety ranges from galloping gospels, to contemporary ballads, from joyful carols to tender manger lullabies.

35028868	SA(T)B	$7.95

TAPESTRY OF LIGHT

A CELTIC CHRISTMAS CELEBRATION

Joseph M. Martin

The joy and hope of Christmas are celebrated in this new Celtic-styled cantata from the pen that brought you *The Mystery and the Majesty* and *Winter's Grace*. This jubilant work is filled with tuneful carols, thoughtful narration, and sparkling orchestrations. Traditional melodies form the foundations of this tapestry of lights bringing to your holiday presentation a pleasing mixture of choirs, carols, and candlelight. Presented in both SAB and SATB formats, a full line of support products is available.

35027955	SAB	$8.95

A CELEBRATION OF CAROLS

Joseph M. Martin

From the composer of *Tapestry of Light* and *The Winter Rose* comes a new major work that is based on the traditional "Lessons and Carols" service. Filled to overflowing with beloved carols and original seasonal songs, this cantata tells the story of Christ's birth adorned with beautiful arrangements and meaningful Scriptures. The work includes optional moments for congregational participation, handbell ringers, and children's choir, if desired. Stunning orchestrations and a full line of support products are available to support your presentation. Titles include: *A Christmas Overture; O Come, All Ye Faithful; A Prayer for Advent; People of Promise, Arise!; Song of Hope and Joy; O Little Town of Bethlehem; My Soul Doth Magnify the Lord; Lullabies of Bethlehem; Angels We Have Heard on High; Carols for Seekers; Let Christmas Begin; A Christmas Trilogy.*

35028358	SAB	$8.95

ACOUSTIC PRAISE

SONGS FOR THE GROWING CHOIR

This helpful choral songbook contains newly composed songs and classics arranged with sensitivity to smaller and developing choirs. Thoughtful SAB voicing makes this useful resource a must-do for slim Sundays and for times when rehearsal times are limited. The acoustic qualities of the arrangements and the optional instrumental obbligatos open this book up to both traditional and contemporary-styled worship ensembles. A variety of subjects and writers are featured and a pleasant track option is available. Titles include: *Come, Walk With Me; The Earth Is the Lord's; Hear Us, O Father; I Will Rejoice and Be Glad; Lord of Life; On Jordan's Stormy Banks; One Day We'll Stand; Train Up a Child; A Choral Benediction.*

35028676	SAB	$7.95
35028677	Listening CD	$15.99
35028678	Preview Pack (SAB Book/Listening CD)	$12.99
35028712	Instrumental Pack CD-ROM	$19.95
35028754	StudioTrax CD	$49.99

Find us on Facebook
Shawnee Press Sacred
www.shawneepress.com

Shawnee Press

HAL•LEONARD®

Prices, contents, and availability
subject to change without notice.

MORE RESOURCES FOR THE DEVELOPING CHOIR

THE SONG EVERLASTING

A SACRED CANTATA BASED ON EARLY AMERICAN SONGS

Joseph Martin

From the composer who brought you *Tapestry of Light*, *The Rose of Calvary* and *The Lenten Sketches*, comes a new work filled with the music of grace. The life of Christ is dramatically presented in this choral cantata that tells the gospel story using American folk songs and hymns. Filled with time-honored tunes and texts, this masterfully arranged work will connect with the congregation and choir alike.

Divided into three sections – Ministry, Humility and Victory – this cantata can be done progressively throughout Lent, Holy Week and Eastertide, or it can be performed as one large celebration of the life of Christ. The miracle and blessing of Christ's earthly ministry, the humility of His passion and the victory of His resurrection fill this work with emotion and power. Thoughtful narration and spectacular orchestrations crown the cantata with variety and skill. Optional moments for congregational participation are included to incorporate your community of faith. A full line of support products is available.

35028163 SAB...$8.95

ONE REHEARSAL WONDERS – VOLUME 1

ALMOST INSTANT ANTHEMS FOR ANY OCCASION

From contemporary chorals for worship, to expressive songs of devotion and praise, this compilation of eight anthems plus bonus benediction is ideal for smaller adult and youth choirs. Includes some of today's leading writers: Pepper Choplin • Michael Barrett • Don Besig and Nancy Price • J. Paul Williams • David Lantz III • Joseph M. Martin • Patty Drennan • and others.

35016264	SATB	$6.95
35016265	Preview Pack (Book/CD)	$16.95
35016266	Listening CD	$15.99
35016267	StudioTrax CD	$49.99
35016269	iPrint Orchestration CD	$39.95

Shawnee Press

HAL•LEONARD®

ONE REHEARSAL WONDERS – VOLUME 2

ALMOST INSTANT ANTHEMS FOR ANY OCCASION

Once again, this second volume delivers joyful songs of worship and soaring anthems of adoration all highly accessible to choirs of all sizes with a minimum of rehearsal time.

Includes: *He Lifted Me* • *The Old Rugged Cross* • *Alleluia, Praise His Name* • *The Everlasting Arms* • *My Savior* • and more.

35016271	SATB	$7.99
35016270	Preview Pack (Book/CD)	$16.99
35016272	Listening CD	$15.98
35016273	StudioTrax CD	$49.95
35016274	iPrint Orchestration CD	$39.95

ONE REHEARSAL WONDERS – VOLUME 3

ALMOST INSTANT ANTHEMS FOR ANY OCCASION

These best sellers are ready when you need them. After *One-Rehearsal Wonders*, *Volumes 1 and 2* were such runaway hits, we felt we had to continue these helpful compilations featuring some of our best sellers adapted for churches with limited rehearsal time. This collection of chorals will provide a steady procession of favorites for your choir and congregation and a great value for your music budget. Don't miss this treasury of 11 proven winners scored for SAB and two-part choirs. Ideal for summer choir repertoire when numbers are lower or for small ensembles any time! Titles include: *The Time for Singing Has Come; I Surrender, Lord; Down By the Riverside; Truly God Is Good; Peace Go with You; Clap Your Hands and Sing Hallelujah;* and more.

35026767	SAB	$7.95
35027062	Preview Pack (Book/CD)	$16.99
35027061	Listening CD	$15.99
35027060	StudioTrax CD	$49.99

SIMPLE SONGS FOR SLIM SUNDAYS

From some of today's top sacred writers comes this collection perfect for anytime you are numbers challenged. Two-part and easy SAB numbers from our archive of best sellers make this a terrific value. Includes: *Come, Thou Fount; Consider the Lilies; Peace Like a River; Come with Shouting; We Bring Our Thanks; Sing Forever to the Lord; A Closing Prayer;* and more.

35020024	2-Part/SAB	$7.95
35020025	SAB Book & Listening CD	$16.95
35020026	Listening CD	$16.99

0313